Our Home
ADDRESS AND NOTEBOOK

LION
Giftlines

Contents

Household members
In an emergency
Daytime contacts
Local information
Don't forget
Household health
Health records
Children's immunization record
Making your voice heard
Finding help from the Bible
National helplines
Address book
Year book

Household members

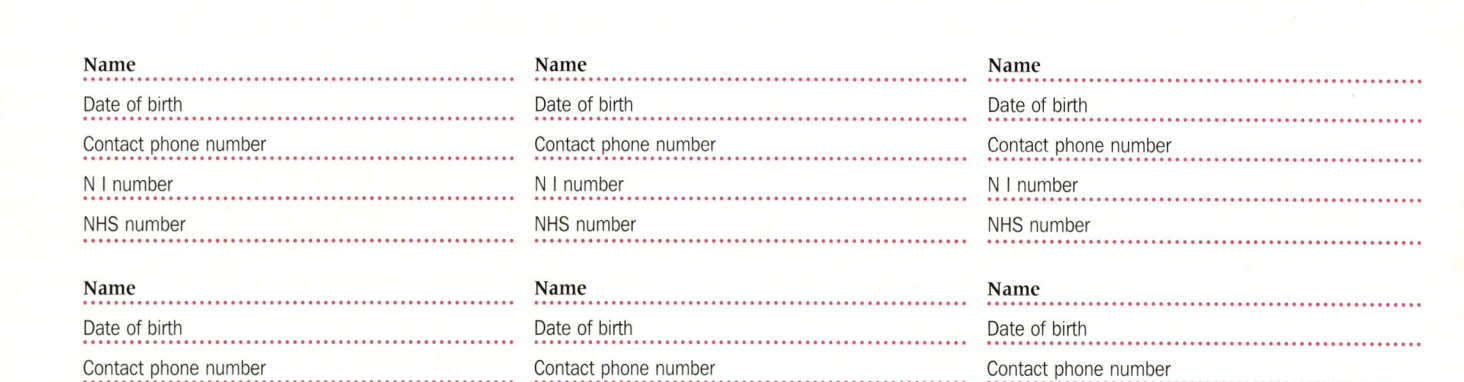

Name

Date of birth

Contact phone number

N I number

NHS number

Name

Date of birth

Contact phone number

N I number

NHS number

Name

Date of birth

Contact phone number

N I number

NHS number

Name

Date of birth

Contact phone number

N I number

NHS number

Name

Date of birth

Contact phone number

N I number

NHS number

Name

Date of birth

Contact phone number

N I number

NHS number

In an emergency

In an emergency

For fire, police, ambulance, coastguard, mountain rescue or cave rescue call:

999

State clearly which service you require

- **Doctor's name**
  Surgery address
  ....
  ....
  Phone
  ....

- **Local emergency hospital**
  Address
  ....
  ....
  Phone
  ....

- **Police station**
  Address
  ....
  ....
  Phone
  ....

- **Next of kin**
  Address
  ....
  ....
  Phone
  ....

- **Neighbour/friend**
  Address
  ....
  ....
  Phone
  ....

- **Electrician**
  Address
  ....
  ....
  Phone
  ....

- **Vet**
  Address
  ....
  ....
  Phone
  ....

- **Emergency numbers**
  Gas ....
  Electricity ....
  Water ....

Where to find:

First Aid supplies & First Aid book

Fire extinguisher/fire blanket

Tool kit

Gas tap *(to turn off supply)*

Gas meter

Electricity mains switch *(to turn off supply)*

Electricity meter

Water stopcock *(to turn off supply)*

Daytime contacts

Name

Contact

Contact address

Department

Phone number

Name

Contact

Contact address

Department

Phone number

Name

Contact

Contact address

Department

Phone number

Name

Contact

Contact address

Department

Phone number

Name

Contact

Contact address

Department

Phone number

Name

Contact

Contact address

Department

Phone number

Local information

- **Doctor's surgery/ health centre**

  Name

  Address of surgery

  GP's name

  Phone

  Surgery hours

  Clinic

  Day/hours

  Clinic

  Day/hours

- **Dental surgery**

  Address of surgery

  Dentist's name

  Phone

  Opening hours

- **Chemist**

  Name

  Opening hours

- **Bank**

  Name

  Branch address

  Phone

  Account number

- **Building society**

  Name

  Branch address

  Phone

  Account number

- **Job centre**

  Address

  Phone

- **Library**

  Opening days/hours:

  Phone

- **Place of worship**

  Address

  Minister

  Phone

  Times of services

- **Recycling site**

  Address

  Hours

- **Rubbish**

  Bin day

  Special collection phone

Housing & social services

• Local Council

Address
....
....

Department
Contact name
Phone

Department
Contact name
Phone

Department
Contact name
Phone

Department
Contact name
Phone

Transport

• Train

Train times past the hour
Last train
Train information phone

• Bus

Bus number
Bus times past the hour
Bus number
Bus times past the hour
Bus station phone

• Taxi

Taxi/minicab phone

Leisure activities

Organization
Contact
Phone
Meeting day
Place

Organization
Contact
Phone
Meeting day
Place

Organization
Contact
Phone
Meeting day
Place

Organization
Contact
Phone
Meeting day
Place

Organization
Contact
Phone
Meeting day
Place

Organization
Contact
Phone
Meeting day
Place

Leisure facilities

Place	Name	Address	Phone booking no	Opening hours
Bowling alley				
Cinema				
Leisure centre				
Skating rink				
Swimming-pool				
Theatre				

Don't forget

Get wisdom and insight! Do not forget or ignore what I say. Do not abandon wisdom, and she will protect you; love her, and she will keep you safe.

From the Book of Proverbs in the Bible

Renewal	Date	Other renewals	Date
TV licence			
Car			
Road fund licence			
MOT			
Service: miles			
Service: miles			
Service: miles			
Service: miles			
Car insurance			
House insurance			
Subs			
Club/society membership			
Magazine			

Household health

It is important to make sure every member of the household is as fit as possible in body, mind and spirit. Here are some generally recommended guidelines.

Eating Well

The body needs a daily intake of protein (supplied by meat, fish, dairy products, beans and eggs), carbohydrates (such as cereals, grains and root vegetables), fats (from oil, animal and dairy products) and fibre (fresh fruit and vegetables). A balanced diet of fresh food should also supply the necessary minerals and vitamins. Avoid too much red meat, fat, white bread, cakes, biscuits, sweets and sweet drinks. Drink semi-skimmed milk and use margarine labelled 'low in saturates'.

To find out if you are entitled to help with health costs, pick up leaflets from your local social security office, or write to the Department of Health, PO Box 410, Wetherby, West Yorkshire LS23 7LN for information.

Getting exercise

An adult needs three 20-minute sessions of regular, vigorous exercise every week and around 8 hours' sleep every night. It is important to find an activity that you enjoy, or you will not continue with it.

Strong-minded

Long after school days, we still need to keep our minds active and interested. There is a wealth of books, tapes and videos available from your local library. Be selective about your TV viewing. Watch programmes that will set you thinking and discuss them with friends and family afterwards.

In good spirits

It is important to have moments of peace, quiet and relaxation in a busy life. The practice of keeping one day in the week for rest and relaxation is an old one which helps to reduce stress and keep work in perspective. Prayer is also a good way to keep in touch with our deepest values.

Medical checks

Regular check-ups at the dentist, optician and at least an annual check-up with your doctor should ensure that any medical problems are recognized and treated in their early stages.

Health records

Name
NHS number
Blood group
Major illnesses

Allergies

Medicines

Next of kin

Name
NHS number
Blood group
Major illnesses

Allergies

Medicines

Next of kin

Name
NHS number
Blood group
Major illnesses

Allergies

Medicines

Next of kin

Name
NHS number
Blood group
Major illnesses

Allergies

Medicines

Next of kin

Name
NHS number
Blood group
Major illnesses

Allergies

Medicines

Next of kin

Name
NHS number
Blood group
Major illnesses

Allergies

Medicines

Next of kin

Children's immunization record

			Child's name	Child's name	Child's name	Child's name
Age	Inoculation	Method	Date of immunization			
2 months	HIB	One injection				
3 months	Diphtheria	One injection				
4 months	Whooping cough/tetanus	One injection				
4 months	Polio	By mouth				
12–15 months	Measles/mumps/rubella	One injection				
3 years	Measles/mumps/rubella	One injection (booster)				
4–5 years	Diphtheria/tetanus	One injection				
Before school	Polio	By mouth				
13 years	Tuberculosis	Test plus injection (BCG—done at school)				
14–15 years	Diphtheria/tetanus	One injection				
14–15 years	Polio	By mouth				

Making your voice heard

Registering to vote

Everyone in a democracy should exercise their vote. Make sure you are registered by contacting the Electoral Registration Department of your local council. The number will be published in the BT phone book, the Local Guide in *Yellow Pages*, or available at your local library.

X

Complaints procedures

First stop
If you have any complaints about the services which Shaftesbury Housing Group supply, consult your tenants handbook.

Advertisements
If you have found an advertisement indecent, dishonest or untruthful, contact: The Advertising Standards Authority, Brook House, Torrington Place, LONDON WC1.

TV and radio
If you have watched a programme on television or listened to one on the radio which you would like to praise or criticize, you will find an address on the letters page of the *Radio Times*.

MP
To write to your MP, address the letter:
c/o The House of Commons, Houses of Parliament, Westminster, LONDON SW1.

The Press
Press complaints are dealt with by: The Press Complaints Commission, 1 Salisbury Square, LONDON EC4.

Finding help from the Bible

Everyone needs somewhere to turn when difficulties arise. Usually it is a friend or counsellor. Sometimes, when there is nobody close to talk to, written advice can be helpful. For centuries the Bible has offered this kind of comfort and encouragement to thousands. So much so that the Gideons, a group of concerned Christian businessmen, make sure that there is a copy of at least the New Testament in every hotel and hostel bedroom. This selected list comes from the notes in the beginning of a Bible produced by the Gideons.

KEY TO BIBLE REFERENCES:

book name/chapter/verses

1 John 1: 5–10

When you are afraid:
Isaiah 41:10; Psalm 56:3,4,10,11; Isaiah 12:2; Mark 4:35–41.

When someone you love has died:
1 Thessalonians 4:13–18; Psalm 147:3; 1 Corinthians 15:51–57; Revelation 21:3–5.

When you have done wrong:
1 John 1:5–10; Psalm 51; Psalm 103:12; Proverbs 28:13; Luke 15:11–24.

When you are at your wits' end:
Psalm 61:1–3; Psalm 55:16,17,22; Psalm 62:1,2; Psalm 94:18,19,22; Psalm 121:1,2,7.

When facing death:
John 3:16; Psalm 23:4; Jonah 2:7–9; John 14:1–3; Revelation 21:4.

When coping with failure:
Psalm 73:26; Psalm 77; Psalm 84:11; Hebrews 4:14–16; Jude 24,25.

When your faith is weak:
Luke 12:22–31; Joshua 1:7–9; Isaiah 7:9; Matthew 8:5–13.

When you feel far from God:
Psalm 145:18; Psalm 42:5–11; Psalm 139:1–18; Acts 17:22–30; James 4:8.

When you feel inadequate:
2 Corinthians 12:9,10; Psalm 138:8;
1 Corinthians 1:20–31; Philippians 4:12,13.

When you feel lost:
Luke 19:10; Psalm 107:4–9; Ephesians 2:12,13.

When you are ill or in pain:
2 Corinthians 12:9,10; Psalm 38:3–10;
Psalm 69:29,30; Psalm 103:1–4; James 5:14–16.

In danger or threatened:
Psalm 118:6–9; Psalm 27:1; Proverbs 18:10;
Mark 4:37–41; 1 Peter 3:13,14.

When you are lonely:
Deuteronomy 31:8; Genesis 28:15;
Psalm 23; Revelation 3:20.

When you are without a job:
Proverbs 16:3–9; Psalm 71:3;
Isaiah 48:17 and 58:9–11; Colossians 3:17,23.

When you need guidance:
Proverbs 3:5,6; Psalm 32:8–10;
Isaiah 48:17,18; Romans 12:1,2.

When you need to find peace:
John 14:27; Isaiah 26:3,4;
Romans 5:1–5; Philippians 4:4–7.

When you wish to pray:
1 John 5:14,15; Psalm 66:17,20;
Luke 11:1–13; John 14:12–14;
James 5:13,16.

When you cannot sleep:
Matthew 11:28; Psalm 3:5 and
4:1,6–8; Proverbs 3:21–26.

When tempted to commit suicide:
Psalm 31:9,14,15; 1 Kings 19:3–5;
Psalm 88:1–5,13; Isaiah 50:10;
1 Corinthians 3:16,17.

When you are being victimized:
Psalm 37:8–11,34; Psalm 59:3,4,9,10;
Proverbs 16:7; Hebrews 13:6.

A copy of the booklet **Bible Helps** *can be obtained from Gideons International, Western House, George Street, Lutterworth, Leicestershire LE17 4EE*

National helplines

In times of crisis, when a listening ear is needed, it is not always easy to talk to a close friend or a member of your family. Telephone helplines ensure that you can talk to an informed person in confidence at any time. Here are some of the main helplines available in the UK:

AIDS
National AIDS Helpline: 0800 567123
Terence Higgins Trust helpline: 0171 242 1010

Alcohol abuse
Alcoholics Anonymous helpline: 0171 352 3001
Al-Anon Family Groups 24hr helpline: 0171 403 0888
The National Alcohol Helpline: 0345 320202
Drinkline Freephone: 0500 801802

Animal welfare
RSPCA (24 hours): 0990 555999
Royal Society for the Preservation of Birds: 01767 680551

Bereavement
Child Death Helpline freefone: 0800 282986
Compassionate Friends (support group for bereaved parents): 0117 953 9639
Cot Death helpline (24 hour): 0171 235 1721
CRUSE Bereavement: 0181 332 7227
Stillbirth & Neonatal Death Society (SANDS): 0171 436 5881

Cancer
Imperial Cancer Research Fund
BACUP Cancer Information Service: 0171 613 2121
Cancer Counselling Service: 0171 696 9000/ 0800 181199
Breast Cancer Campaign freeline: 0500 245345

Children
Childline freefone (24 hours): 0800 1111
NSPCC Child Protection Helpline (24hr freefone): 0800 800500

Consumer advice
Office of Fair Trading consumer information line: 0345 224499

Trading Standards Departments: see under Local Authority in your phone book

Counselling
National Association of Citizens Advice Bureaux: 0171 251 2000

Careline (telephone counselling service): 0181 514 1177

Debt
Credit Action Helpline: 0800 591084

National Debtline: 0121 359 8501

Disability
Carers Line: 0171 490 8898

DIAL UK Disability Helpline: 01302 310123

Disabled Living Foundation: 0171 289 6111

Royal Association for Disability and Rehabilitation (RADAR): 0171 250 3222

Domestic violence
Women's Aid National Helpline: 0117 963 3542

Drugs
Family Drugs Charity (Adfam) national helpline: 0171 638 3700

Narcotics Anonymous Helpline: 0171 730 0009

Release Drugs Advice Line: 0171 729 9904

(24 hr emergency): 0171 603 8654

Turning Point: 0171 720 2300

Eating disorders
Anorexics Anonymous (anorexia and bulimia): 0181 878 9199

Eating Disorders Association: 01603 621414

Elderly
Age Concern: 0181 679 8000

Family
Families Anonymous: 0171 498 4680

Gingerbread (for lone parents): 0171 336 8184

National Council for One Parent Families: 0171 267 1361

Gambling
Gamblers Anonymous (24 hour): 0171 384 3040

Homosexuality
London Lesbian and Gay Switchboard (24 hour): 0171 837 7324

Marriage guidance
Relate: 0181 445 9549/0888

Mental health
Mencap: 0171 454 0454
MIND (National Association for Mental Health): 0181 519 2122
SANELINE (for friends & family of people with mental illness): 0345 678 000

Missing persons
National Missing Persons Helpline (24 hr) for advice: 0500 700 700
Message home (no questions asked): 0500 700 740
Salvation Army Family Tracing Service: 0171 383 2772

Pregnancy advice
Brook Advisory Centre (24 hour helpline): 0171 617 8000
LIFE hotline: 01926 311511
National Childbirth Trust: 0181 992 8637

Rape and sexual abuse
Rape Crisis Centre: 0171 837 1600

Refugees
Refugee Council Advice Line: 0171 582 9927

Someone to talk to
The Samaritans (24 hour line): 0345 909090

Smoking
Quit (helping smokers to stop) freefone: 0800 002200

Social security
Freeline Social Security (for benefit, pensions and National Insurance advice): 0800 666555 (also check the telephone directory for your local social security office)

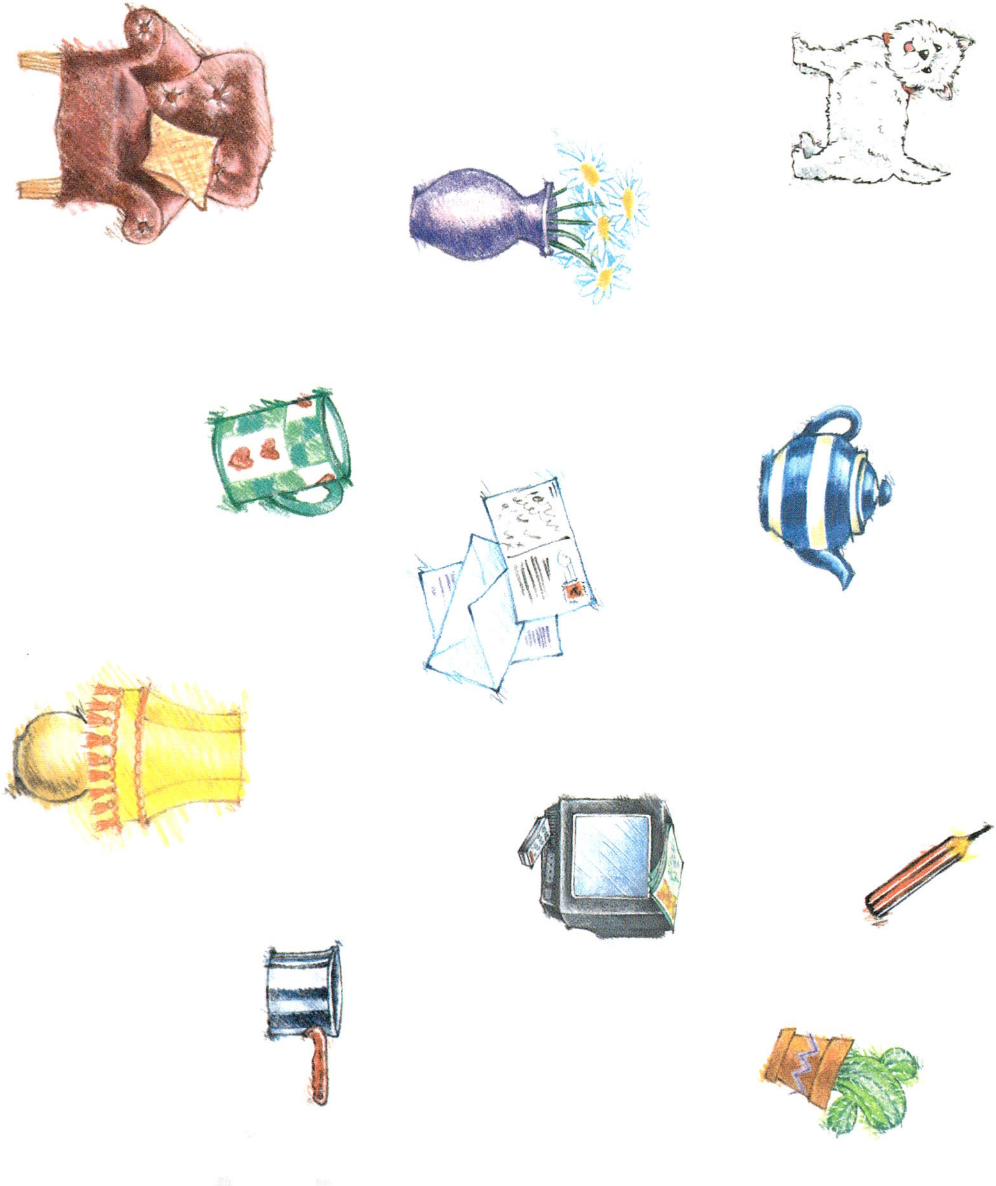

Address book

A

Name　　　　　　　　　　　　　Address　　　　　　　　　　　　　　　　　　　　　　　　Phone number

Home is where the heart is.

Name	Address	Phone number

B

Some friends play at friendship but a true friend sticks closer than one's nearest kin.

The Book of Proverbs

C

Name **Address** **Phone number**

> Happy is he who like Ulysses has made a great journey, or like that man who won the Fleece and then came home, full of experience and good sense, to live the rest of his time among his family.
>
> Joachim Du Bellay

Name   Address   Phone number

D

Keep far our foes, give peace at home: Where Thou art guide, no ill can come.

Book of Common Prayer

E

Home is where you can find your way in the dark.

Name   Address   Phone number

Name Address Phone number

F

> Happiness is to be found only in the home where God is loved and honoured, where each one loves, and helps, and cares for the others.
>
> Theophanes Vénard

G

Name	Address	Phone number

Mid pleasures and palaces though we may we roam,
Be it ever so humble, there's no place like home.

J.H Payne

Name	Address	Phone number

H

Better a dry crust with peace and quiet than a house full of feasting with strife.

The Book of Proverbs

I

Name	Address	Phone number

There are many rooms in my Father's house, and I am going to prepare a place for you.

Jesus, in John's Gospel

Name   Address   Phone number

J

> Have nothing in your home that you do not know to be useful or believe to be beautiful.
>
> **William Morris**

K

Name　　　**Address**　　　**Phone number**

Blessed are the peacemakers: for they shall be called the children of God.

From the Beatitudes in Matthew's Gospel

Name	Address	Phone number

L

The best and most beautiful things in the world cannot be seen or touched but are felt in the heart.

Helen Keller

M

Name Address Phone number

> There's no place like home.
> There's no place like home.
> There's no place like home.
>
> **Dorothy in** *The Wizard of Oz*

Name Address Phone number

N

To see a world in
a grain of sand,
And heaven in a
wild flower,
Hold infinity in
the palm of
your hand,
And eternity in
an hour.

William Blake

O

Name   Address   Phone number

It is a most miserable thing to feel ashamed of home.

Charles Dickens

Name   Address   Phone number

P

Whatever possessions you hold in this world—hold them with an open hand.

Corrie Ten Boom

Q R

Name **Address** **Phone number**

Friendship is a sheltering tree.

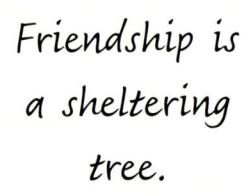

Samuel Taylor Coleridge

Name Address Phone number **S**

Friendship is
love with
understanding.

Proverb

Name	Address	Phone number

T

The kingdom of God is within you.

Jesus, in Luke's Gospel

| Name | Address | Phone number | # U V W |

I thank my God for you every time I think of you.

From the Letter to the Philippians

x y z

Name　　　　　　　　　　Address　　　　　　　　　　　　　　　　　　　　　　　Phone number

> Listen, I stand at the door and knock; if anyone hears my voice and opens the door, I will come in and eat with them, and they will eat with me.

Jesus, in the Book of Revelation

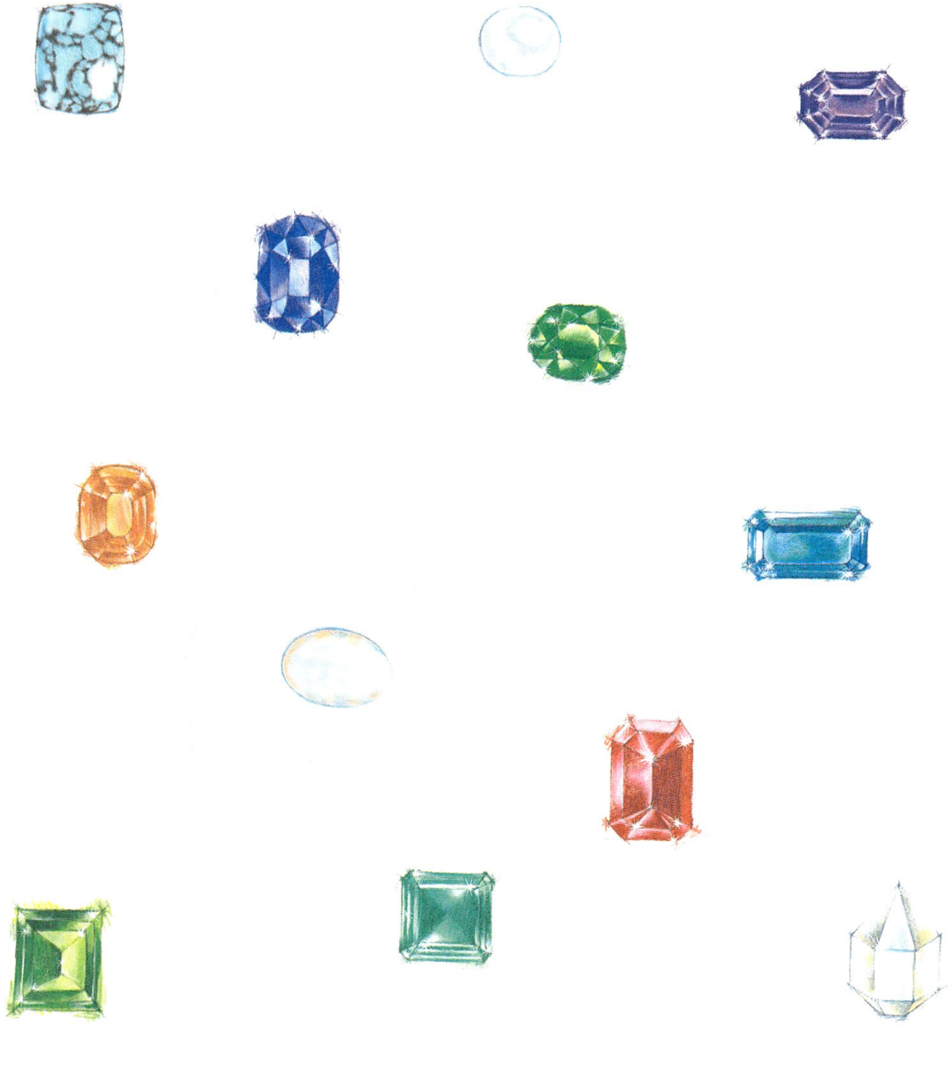

Yearbook

In January

*God be here, God be there,
We wish you all a happy year;
God without, God within,
Let the Old Year out
and the New Year in.*

Traditional rhyme

Special days

1st: New Year's Day

6th: Epiphany Christian festival commemorating the arrival of the wise men to see the baby Jesus.

6th: Twelfth night after Christmas When decorations should be taken down.

25th: Burn's Night Festival in honour of Scotland's national poet, Robert Burns.

Chinese New Year A week-long festival between January 21st and February 20th.

Birthdays

January's birthstone is green garnet

Things to do in January

- List what you hope to achieve this year. Decide on your first step towards each goal.
- Write to or phone friends and relations who sent you Christmas cards.
- Have a 'swap party' where everyone brings their unwanted gifts and clothes to give away.

With children

Make shaped biscuits:

- Draw and cut out simple shapes in cardboard. (You could make the star that brought the wise men to see the baby Jesus.)
- Make some biscuit dough and roll out.
- Help children to cut round the shapes.
- Lay biscuits on a baking tray and cook.
- Decorate with coloured icing.

In February

*If Candlemas Day be fair and bright
Winter will take another flight.
If Candlemas Day be cloud and rain
Winter is gone and
will not come again*

Traditional rhyme

Special days

2nd: Candlemas When candles are blessed for use in churches throughout the year.

14th: St Valentine's Day, patron saint of lovers When cards and flowers are sent.

29th Once every four years February has an extra 'leap year' day added.

Purim Jewish feast celebrates the defeat of the Persian tyrant Haman by Queen Esther. Poppyseed buns and 'Haman's ears'—triangular fritters sprinkled with sugar—are eaten.

Holi Hindu spring festival.

Birthdays

February's birthstone is amethyst

Things to do in February

- Learn to make your own candles.
- Make a home-made Valentine card.
- Bake some poppyseed buns.

With children

Make heart baskets for Valentine's Day:
- Fold a red and a yellow piece of paper in half.
- Cut out these shapes.

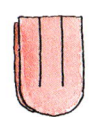

- Make two cuts from folded edges.
- Push first red strip between first yellow, open it and slot it over second yellow and then between third.
- Open second red and slot it over first yellow, between second and over third yellows.
- Push third red between, over and between.
- This process needs a bit of practice, but when you have it right the heart shape will open to form a basket to hold a gift.

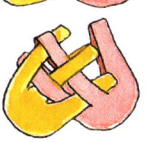

In March

Mix a pancake, stir a pancake,
Pop it in the pan.
Fry a pancake, toss a pancake,
Catch it if you can.

Traditional rhyme

Special days

1st: St David's Day Bishop and patron saint of Wales.

17th: St Patrick's Day Celtic missionary and patron saint of Ireland.

Mothering Sunday/Mother's Day Originally a day to celebrate the 'Mother Church' or the local parish on the 4th Sunday of Lent, this day has evolved into a special day for mothers.

Shrove Tuesday Popularly known as Pancake Day. This is the day when Christians use up the rich food before the season of Lent, a period of fasting before Easter.

Ash Wednesday The first day of Lent; the forty-day Christian fast in preparation for Easter.

Ramadan Beginning of 40-day period of fasting for Muslims to commemorate Mohammed's receiving of the Koran.

Birthdays

March's birthstone is jasper, bloodstone or aquamarine

Things to do in March

■ Plant daffodil bulbs in window-boxes, or under grass, for a surprise next year.
■ During Lent, read a modern version of the New Testament.
■ Make leek soup in honour of St David.

With children

Make pancakes.
You will need:

150g self-raising flour
25g butter
25g caster sugar
2 eggs, 400 ml milk
Butter for frying

● Put everything into a blender and whiz until as thick as cream (or beat in a bowl with a whisk)
● Melt a little butter in a frying pan.
● Pour in a tablespoonful of mixture.
● Cook for a minute, then flip the pancake over with a spatula and cook the second side.
● Keep pancakes warm while you make more.

In April

> Hot cross buns! Hot cross buns!
> One a penny, two a penny,
> Hot cross buns!
>
> Street vendor's song

Special days

1st: April Fool's Day In Europe, a day to play tricks on others.

23rd: St George's Day Patron saint of England and legendary dragonslayer.

The season of Easter includes **Palm Sunday** the weekend beforehand, when Jesus entered the city of Jerusalem riding a donkey. **Good Friday** is the day on which Jesus was crucified. Three days later, his resurrection is celebrated on **Easter Day**.

Pesach/Passover Jewish festival commemorating the exodus of the Israelites from Egypt. No yeast or flour is allowed in the house during the week and a special meal is eaten by all the family.

Birthdays

April's birthstone is a sapphire or diamond

Things to do in April

■ When boiling eggs, surprise everyone by drawing faces on them first with an indelible marker.

■ Look for signs of new life in the plants and wildlife around you.

■ Invite your extended family round for a meal.

With children

Make a spring or Easter garden (it will take 4–5 weeks to grow):

- Mix some potting compost with grass seeds.
- Lay half of the compost in the bottom of a shallow dish.
- Lay a flowerpot on its side in the centre, to form a cave or tomb.
- Pour the rest of the compost into an old stocking and lay it over the flowerpot.
- Add small plants round the edge or bury small water jars to hold cut flowers.
- Water every few days until the grass has grown.
- Make an Easter scene by adding small wooden crosses and a round stone.

In May

Here we come gathering nuts in May,
Nuts in May, nuts in May,
Here we come gathering nuts in May,
On a cold and frosty morning.
Children's rhyme

Special days

1st: May Day The first of May has long been associated with the countryside and dancing round the maypole.

International Labour Day In honour of workers.

Ascension Day Forty days after Easter, Ascension Day celebrates Jesus' return to Heaven to be with his Father.

Shavuoth/Pentecost Jewish festival remembering the giving of the Torah on Sinai. The Ten Commandments are read in the synagogue.

Pentecost/Whitsunday Christian festival marking the coming of the Holy Spirit on the first Christians.

Birthdays

May's birthstone is agate or emerald

Things to do in May

■ Grow some herbs in a flowerpot in the kitchen.
■ Put up chimes, or ribbons so that you can enjoy a windy day.
■ Get some outdoor exercise. Go swimming, or take a walk in the park.

With children

Fly a kite.
● Fold a large sheet of stiff paper in half.
● Fold both points down over a ruler as shown.
● Tape a straw to the back.
● Tape three 2-metre lengths of gift ribbon together in the middle.
● Punch a hole in the bottom of the kite and tie the tassel to it with strong cotton.
● Tie a ball of cotton to a paper-clip and tape it near the top. To fly the kite in a light breeze, run into the wind pulling the kite and it will fly up behind you.

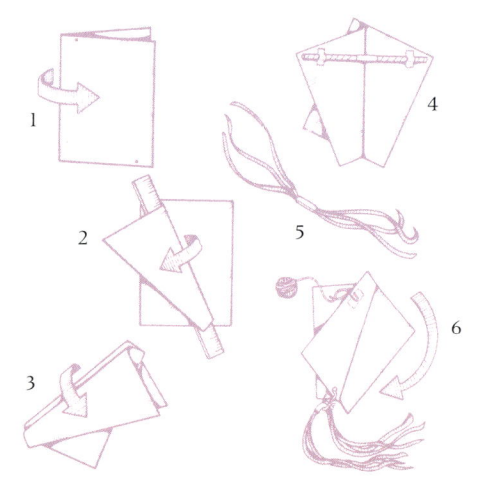

1
2
3
4
5
6

In June

*June brings tulips, lilies, roses,
Fills the children's hands with posies.*
— Sara Coleridge

Special days

Midsummer's Day The longest day of the year in the Northern Hemisphere, when the sun is at its farthest from the equator.

3rd Sunday: Father's Day in the UK & USA.

Birthdays

June's birthstone is emerald, pearl or moonstone

Things to do in June

■ Think of something helpful to do for your father or another relative.

■ Get up early on Midsummer morning and enjoy the longest day of the year.

■ Cool down with a milkshake made from 1/2 pint milk, 2 tablespoons of chocolate syrup and 2 tablespoons of crushed ice.

With children

Make a delicious summer fruit boat:

● Cut a honeydew melon into wedges.

● Scoop out the seeds with a teaspoon.

● Wash some strawberries, cut them in half and remove the green stalk and 'core'.

● Arrange the strawberries in a row along the melon wedge to look like colourful rowers in a boat.

In July

St Swithin's Day if thou dost rain,
For forty days it doth remain.
St. Swithin's Day if thou be fine,
For forty days the sun will shine.
Traditional rhyme

Things to do in July
- Go singin' in the rain.
- Plan a 4th July American picnic, with hamburgers, chips and cola.

With children
If you're going to the park or beach, make a stone or shell collection:
- Gather as many different shapes as you can find.
- Wash them carefully and rinse out any sand. They can be displayed in a dish of water.
- Add some salt to keep the water clear.
- Shells can also be used to decorate a box as a gift.
- Glue them to the lid in a pattern and add a coat of varnish.

Special days

4th: American Independence Day Anniversary of the Declaration of Independence from Britain.

14th: Bastille Day, France. Fêtes, processions and banquets take place throughout France to celebrate the French Revolution.

15th: St Swithin's Day Bishop of Winchester in 852. Tradition says that if it rains on this day, it will continue to rain for forty days.

Birthdays

July's birthstone is onyx or ruby

In August

> To every thing there is a season, and a time to every purpose under the heaven.
>
> **The Book of Ecclesiastes**

Special days

1st: Lammas Day Early Harvest Festival, when a loaf of bread was baked from the first ripe grain.

12th: The Glorious Twelfth The grouse-shooting season begins in Britain.

Birthdays

August's birthstone is carnelian, sardonyx or peridot

Things to do in August

■ Re-read a favourite book or magazine.

■ Make real blackcurrant ice-cream. Crush the juices from 1lb berries, add 8oz icing sugar and the juice of 1/2 a lemon. Whisk 1/2 pt double cream until thick and fold into mixture. Pour into a plastic tub and freeze for a few hours.

With children

Do some painting or stencilling. The simplest stencils are made by cutting a paper flower pattern.

- Cut a small circle of paper.
- Fold it in half, then into thirds.
- Cut small pieces from the folded edges and the outer edge.
- Open it up and lay it on a sheet of paper.
- Using a sponge or stencil brush, dab paint all round the shape.
- Lift it off to see the pattern.

In September

If you wait until the wind and the weather are just right, you will never sow anything and never harvest anything.

Wisdom from the Book of Ecclesiastes

Special days

29th: Michaelmas. Feast day of St. Michael and all angels, traditional beginning of university autumn terms.

Jewish New Year begins with the family meal of Rosh Hashanah. Yom Kippur, the Day of Atonement, comes ten days after New Year and Succoth, celebrating the harvest, comes five days later.

Birthdays

September's birthstone is chrysolite or sapphire

Things to do in September

■ Join an evening class.
■ Freshen your rooms by piling some pot-pourri in a bowl or lighting a scented candle.

With children

Make a cardboard basket. This simple basket would hold fruit and vegetables for a harvest festival service or a gift.

● Draw and cut out a cross shape on a large piece of card.
● Using a craft knife, carefully cut three of the cross pieces into four strips and one into five strips, as shown.
● Bend the strips up to form the basket.
● Tape string into one corner and weave it in and out of the strips to the top and tape the end inside.

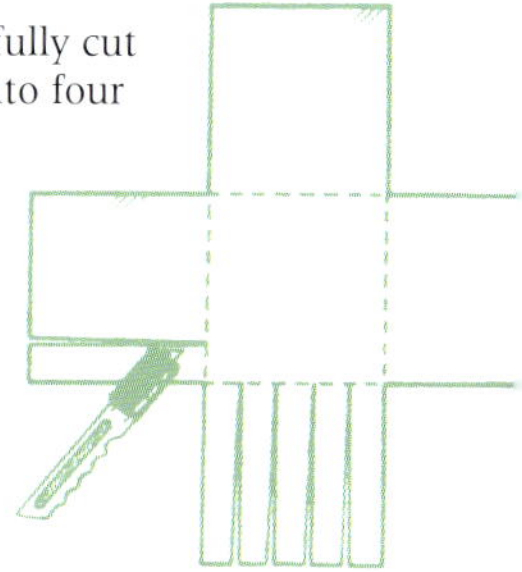

In October

As long as the world exists, there will be a time for planting and a time for harvest. There will always be cold and heat, summer and winter, day and night.

From the Book of Genesis

Special days

Harvest Festival Christian thanksgiving for harvest is usually held on the Sunday nearest to the 1st of October.

31st: Hallowe'en An ancient festival of the dead, when evil spirits were said to walk the earth. Today, children dressed as ghosts and ghouls visit neighbours for a 'trick or treat'.

Divali: Hindu Festival of Lights in honour of Vishnu.

Birthdays

October's birthstone is aquamarine, opal or tourmaline

Things to do in October

■ Clear out your unwanted possessions and take them to a charity shop or give them to friends.

■ Buy some sweets ready for children who come 'trick or treating'.

With children

Make a garden of lights:
- Fill a deep dish with damp sand.
- Push coloured candles into the sand and surround them with glass marbles, shells and stones. These will help to keep them upright and catch the light as they burn. (Do not leave burning candles unattended.)

In November

*Remember, remember, the fifth of November,
Gunpowder, treason and plot.*
Traditional rhyme

Things to do in November
- Buy a poppy to wear for Remembrance Sunday.
- Write to or phone a friend you haven't been in touch with for years.
- Shop early for Christmas!

With children
Make home-made burgers for a bonfire party:
- Peel and chop an onion.
- Beat an egg with a fork.
- Mix these two with 450g ground beef. Season.
- Form into 4 flat burgers.
- Brush with oil and grill for about 5 minutes on each side.
- Have sliced tomatoes, grated cheese, pickles, sauces and buns ready for the children to assemble their own burgers.

Special days

1st: All Saints/All Hallows Day A Christian remembrance day for all the saints.

2nd: All Souls Day Roman Catholic day of prayer for the souls of the departed. In Mexico this is designated the Day of the Dead.

5th: Guy Fawkes Night Fireworks and bonfires commemorate the attempt to blow up the British Houses of Parliament in 1605.

Remembrance Day In UK & Canada, Veterans' Day in USA. The Sunday nearest to the 11th November. Commemoration of war veterans, particularly of the First and Second World Wars. Also known as Poppy Day because poppies made by ex-servicemen are worn as a mark of respect. Two minutes' silence are kept at 11am.

30th: St Andrew's Day Patron saint of Scotland.

Birthdays
The November birthstone is topaz

In December

Unto us a child is born!
King of all creation.
Came into a world forlorn,
The Lord of every nation.
Christmas carol

Special days

Advent The four Sundays leading up to Christmas.

Chanukkah/Hanukkah 8-day Jewish Festival of Lights. A candle is lit and presents are distributed each day.

6th: The Feast of St Nicholas Bishop of Myra in Turkey. His Dutch name is Santa Claus. In Europe, he appears as a bishop with his assistant Black Peter, bringing gifts and encouraging children to be good.

24th: Christmas Eve The night before Christmas

25th: Christmas Day A family day of celebration, present-giving and feasting to celebrate the birth of Jesus Christ.

26th: Boxing Day A public holiday in Commonwealth countries. The name comes from a Christmas Box, or gift of money given to employees.

31st: New Year's Eve The end of the old year and start of the new. On the stroke of midnight in the United Kingdom, people link arms and sing Robert Burns' song, 'Auld Lang Syne'.

31st: Hogmanay Scottish celebration of New Year's Eve.

Birthdays

December's birthstone is ruby, turquoise or zircon

Things to do in December

■ Light a candle each Sunday before dinner and say a prayer.
■ Help distribute food and clothing to local homeless people. 
■ Invite your neighbours to your home to meet one another. Ask them to bring some food to share.
■ Go carol singing with a local group for charity.

With children

Make some special stockings for Christmas morning:

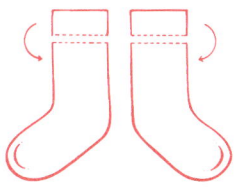

● Fold a piece of felt in half, mark out a stocking shape and cut it out.
● Use felt in a different colour to cut two pieces for the tops.
● With coloured thread, sew the tops to the stockings with a pattern of stitches.
● Finally, sew all round the edge, leaving the top open.

Prayers for our home

Father of all mankind, make the roof of my house wide
enough for all opinions, oil the door of my house so it opens
easily to friend and stranger and set such a table in my house
that my whole family may speak kindly and freely around it.
Amen.
Prayer from Hawaii

Be Christ's cross on your new hearth,
Be Christ's cross on your new abode,
Upon your new fire blazing.
Be Christ's cross on your means and portion.
Be Christ's cross on your kin and people.
Be Christ's cross on you each light and darkness,
Each day and each night of your lives.
A Celtic blessing

God bless our home.
A blessing from Jordan

*If there is righteousness in the heart,
there will be beauty in the character.
If there is beauty in the character,
there will be harmony in the home.
If there is harmony in the home,
there will be order in the nation.
When there is order in each nation,
there will be peace in the world.*

Chinese Proverb